DISCOVER Sound

by Vickey Herold

Table of Contents

Introduction 2
Chapter 1 What Makes Sound? 4
Chapter 2 How Do Vibrations Become Sounds? 8
Chapter 3 Why Is Sound Important? 14
Conclusion 18
Concept Map 20
Glossary 22
Index 24

Introduction

Sound is **vibrations**. Sound is **energy** people hear. Sound is important to people.

▲ Sound is important to people.

Words to Know

 communicate

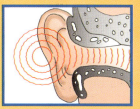 ear

 energy

 sound

 sound waves

 vibrations

See the Glossary on page 22.

Chapter 1
What Makes Sound?

Vibrations make sound.

vibrations

▲ Vibrations are sound.

Sound waves make sound.

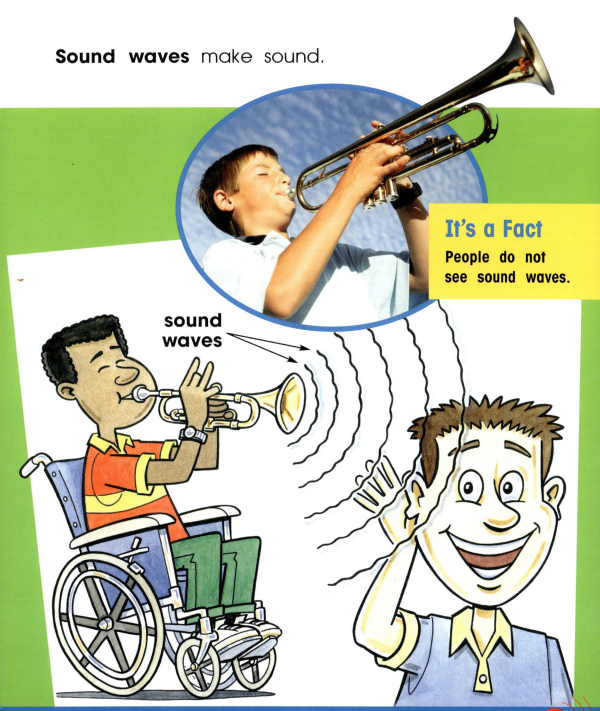

It's a Fact
People do not see sound waves.

sound waves

▲ Sound waves are sound.

Chapter 1

Strong vibrations make loud sounds.

▲ Some vibrations are loud sounds.

Weak vibrations make quiet sounds.

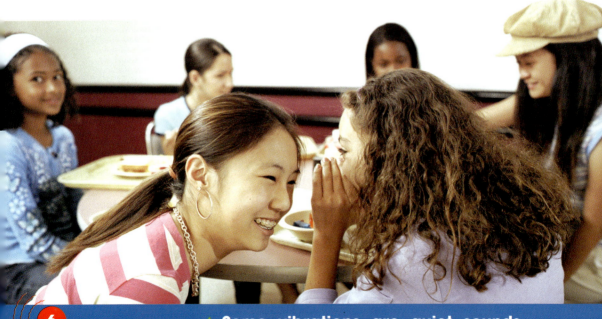

▲ Some vibrations are quiet sounds.

What Makes Sound?

Fast vibrations make high sounds. Whistles make high sounds.

▲ Fast vibrations are high sounds.

Slow vibrations make low sounds. Big drums make low sounds.

▲ Slow vibrations are low sounds.

Chapter 2
How Do Vibrations Become Sounds?

Vibrations move through the air.

▲ Vibrations travel through the air.

Vibrations move to the **ear**.

▲ Vibrations travel to the ear.

Vibrations move into the ear.

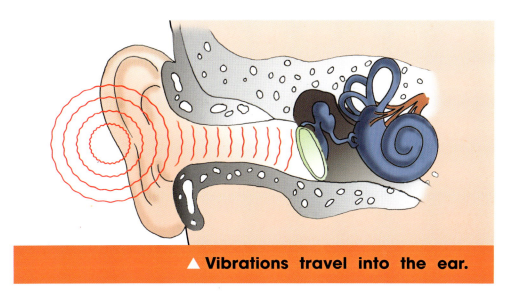

▲ **Vibrations travel into the ear.**

Vibrations move to the eardrum.

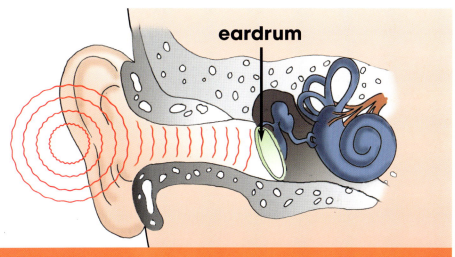

▲ **Vibrations travel to the eardrum.**

Chapter 2

Vibrations move to tiny bones.

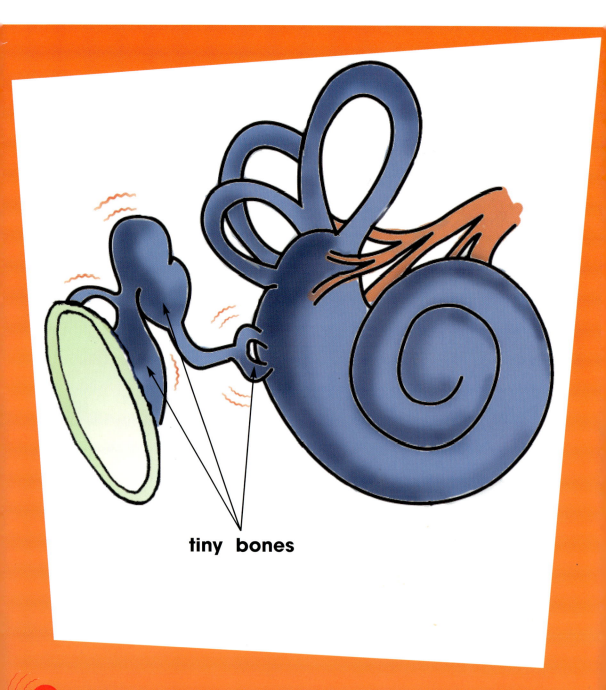

tiny bones

▲ **Vibrations travel to tiny bones.**

How Do Vibrations Become Sounds?

Vibrations move through a tube.

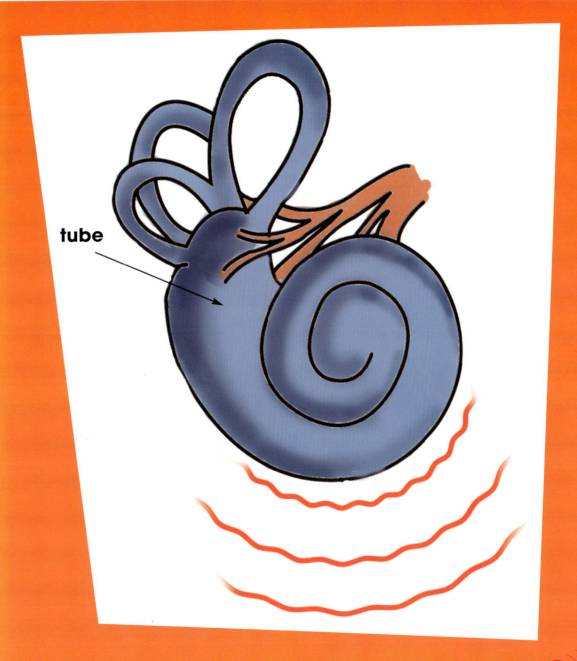

▲ Vibrations travel through a tube.

Chapter 2

Vibrations move to nerves. Vibrations move through the nerves.

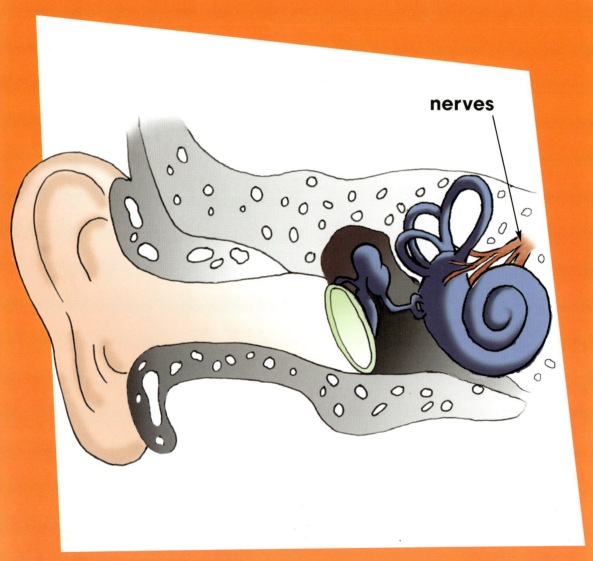

▲ **Vibrations travel through nerves.**

How Do Vibrations Become Sounds?

Vibrations move to the brain.

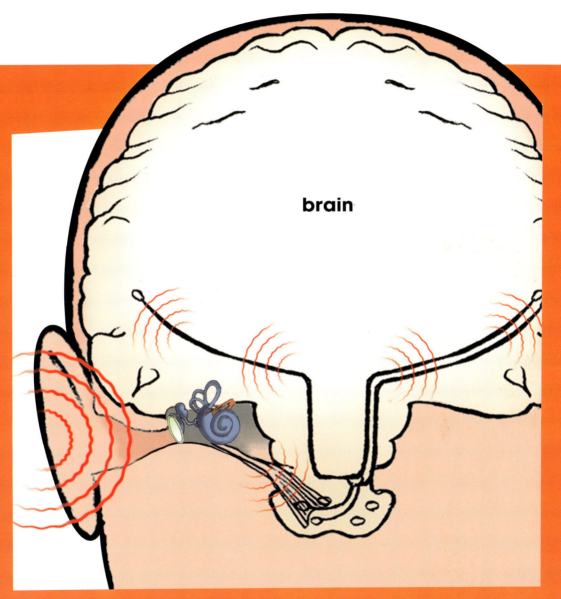

▲ Vibrations travel to the brain.

It's a Fact
Our brains make vibrations into sounds. Our brains make us hear.

Chapter 3

Why Is Sound Important?

People use sound to **communicate**.

▲ Sound helps people communicate.

People use sound to talk.

▲ Sound helps people talk.

People use sound to listen.

▲ Sound helps people listen.

Chapter 3

People use sound to communicate danger.

▲ Sound helps people communicate danger.

People use sound to stay safe.

It's a Fact
Sirens are in many cities. Sirens are very loud noises. Sirens warn people.

▲ Sound helps people stay safe.

Why Is Sound Important?

People use sound to celebrate.

▲ **Sound helps people celebrate.**

Conclusion

Sound is vibrations. Sound is energy that people hear. Sound is important to people.

▲ Sound is important to people.

Concept Map

Sound

What Makes Sound?

- vibrations
- sound waves
- strong vibrations
- weak vibrations
- fast vibrations
- slow vibrations

How Do Vibrations Become Sounds?

- move through air
- move to the ear
- move into the ear
- move to the eardrum
- move to tiny bones
- move through a tube
- move through nerves
- move to the brain

Why Is Sound Important?

to communicate
to talk
to listen
to communicate danger
to stay safe
to celebrate

Glossary

communicate to share information

*People use sound to **communicate**.*

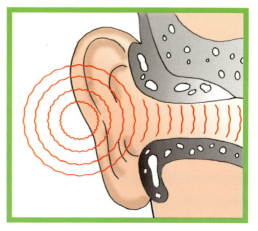

ear body part that helps people hear

*Vibrations move to the **ear**.*

energy power

*Sound is **energy** people hear.*

sound energy that people hear

***Sound** is important to people.*